THE ACENTOS
BOOK PRIZE

2022
WINNER

ALL
WOMEN
ARE
BORN
WAILING

"*All Women Are Born Wailing* is filled with shards of violence woven with threads of memorable beauty. Ramirez's writing evokes a deep, familiar pain in poems that are original and profound. This is the kind of collection you will wish to slowly savor but can't help devouring. A collection meant to be read and reread and recommended to everyone you know."

SHANNON MCLEOD

author of *Whimsy* and *Nature Trail Stories*

"*All Women Are Born Wailing* is an anthology of infinite nuance. It's heart-breaking. It's witty. It's endearing. It's scathing. It's youthful. It's thousands of years in the making. The only thing more impressive than its gradation is its consistency. Every poem is a knockout. There are lines from it that will stick with me for decades. I had to read the entire thing standing up.

Nen G Ramirez can say a thousand words with just a few. One of the truly great poetic voices of our generation."

KYLE PRUE

author of *The Feud* trilogy
writer/creator/producer of
the mini-series, *Rabbit*

"Poems like running red lights, like lightning held long after it strikes, like fire to harrow memory; this, and much more, you'll find in Nen G Ramirez's All Women Are Born Wailing, a magnificent collection that is at once intimate and universal, provocative and celebratory, unafraid to raise a verbal fist against the monsters of cultural stereotypes and expectations. Read these poems, for they'll reassure you that sometimes to keep on living you have to 'outrun [your] blood,' you have to 'outlive [your] weeping name.' And sometimes, this is all that matters."

OCTAVIO QUINTANILLA

author of *If I Go Missing*
San Antonio Poet Laureate 2018–2020

NOMADIC PRESS

OAKLAND

PHILADELPHIA

XALAPA

WWW.NOMADICPRESS.ORG

MASTHEAD

FOUNDING PUBLISHER
J. K. Fowler

ASSOCIATE AND LEAD EDITOR
Michaela Mullin

DESIGN
Jevohn Tyler Newsome

MISSON STATEMENT Through publications, events, and active community participation, Nomadic Press collectively weaves together platforms for intentionally marginalized voices to take their rightful place within the world of the written and spoken word. Through our limited means, we are simply attempting to help right the centuries' old violence and silencing that should never have occurred in the first place and build alliances and community partnerships with others who share a collective vision for a future far better than today.

INVITATIONS Nomadic Press wholeheartedly accepts invitations to read your work during our open reading period every year. To learn more or to extend an invitation, please visit: www.nomadic-press.org/invitations

DISTRIBUTION
Orders by teachers, libraries, trade bookstores, or wholesalers:

Nomadic Press Distribution
orders@nomadicpress.org
(510) 500-5162

Small Press Distribution
spd@spdbooks.org
(510) 524-1668 / (800) 869-7553

This book was made possible by a loving community of chosen family and friends, old and new. For author questions or to book a reading at your bookstore, university/school, or alternative establishment, please send an email to info@nomadicpress.org.

Cover art by Inocencia Ramirez-Gorski
Author portrait by Arthur Johnstone

Published by Nomadic Press, 1941 Jackson Street, Suite 20, Oakland, CA 94612
First printing, 2023

Library of Congress Cataloging-in-Publication Data

Title: *All Women are Born Wailing*
p. cm.
Summary: Nen G Ramirez's *All Women are Born Wailing* confronts myriad forms of violence against Latinas. Drawing on personal and family experiences with mental illness, the poet challenges the "crazy Latina" stereotype and examines the ways it has been used to belittle and dehumanize people who deserve treatment and care. Unflinching in their critique of sexist and racist tropes, in these poems Ramirez experiments with persona and familial history, including the murder of a cousin, in order to imagine more hopeful futures.

[1. POETRY / American / Hispanic & Latino. 2. POETRY / LGBTQ+. 3. POETRY / Subjects & Themes / Death, Grief, Loss. 4. POETRY / General.]

LIBRARY OF CONGRESS CONTROL NUMBER: 2022951450
ISBN: 978-1-955239-52-3

ALL
WOMEN
ARE
BORN
WAILING

ALL WOMEN ARE BORN WAILING

NEN G RAMIREZ

NOMADIC PRESS

Oakland · Philadelphia · Xalapa

for Lora

CONTENTS

reading guide

FOREWORD

Nen Ramirez knows who you think they are. Who you think they should be. What you think they should want. They know because they've paid attention. Marked every wicked cautionary myth and makeup ad, every televised and private trauma, every wrong name and leer you called "flirtation." Nen studied each of these expectations and insistences streamed, thrust, or cooed at them, recording each in their memory. And when we come to find ourselves in the hands of fortune and doom, Nen turns those records into poems. Fortune because we are there, in the grip of a poet who doesn't wish to coddle us even as they'd rather not visit harm upon us. Doomed because this poetry, Nen's poetry, will find us out. It will hunt up the exes crouched in us deep, the pyromaniacs fidgeting in our darkness, the ghosts that lurk in our grief and hunger, the piojos that gorge us with an intimate's blood. *All Women Are Born Wailing*, then, is a hunting call blown through the "carved and hollowed" body of Nen Ramirez, a body this remarkable poet themselves has tried to kill, keen student of the destruction streamed, thrust, and cooed at them. For in this book, Nen first hunts Nen. Still, poetry, like a vein, can be a "bulging pained prayer, a song," and these poems are filled with that which the poet could not forget, could not ever unlearn. Thus, *All Women Are Born Wailing* is also a lesson; a lesson aimed at those who teach through fear and shame, through neglect and cruelty, weapons and weaponized piety.

Here, you'll learn what withdrawal means, why a woman will weep, the composition of a chucked heart, and who the devil is. You will learn these things through poems that entangle lightning strike narrative and vivisectional lyric to forcefully remind us that what we call History is a story strained through "fistfuls of...long dark hair." Fistfuls. Read the violence of "fist-," the plunder of taking things by the "fistful," the synecdoche of "long dark hair" for brown femmes. Read it to know you know it. For Nen wants you to know what they cannot unlearn. And for those already possessed of this harsh knowledge, Nen offers a swollen, agonized entreaty, a new ever sung song. *All Women Are Born Wailing* is this caustic prayer and coruscating song. It scars the throat with its telling. It tolls you to know. It will hunt your hollow and reverberate.

Douglas Kearney

author of *Sho* and *Optic Subwoof*

INTRODUCTION

In 1983, my 11-year-old cousin Lora was sexually assaulted and murdered walking home from a friend's house. She was buried in the cemetery down the street from my childhood home. She was so pretty that the words *Miss America* were written on her headstone. The women in my family told me and my primas the story about Lora's death like a bedtime story, a legend, a warning. A warning against being out alone, against being too visible or too public or too fast.

Growing up was always spoken about like a curse in my family. Growing into a Latina body that would be hypersexualized, it was hard to see it as anything but. The curses for the women in my family were abundant. Anxiety, depression, and bipolar disorder runs in our family through genetics. PTSD runs in our family through shared experience: sexual abuse, physical abuse, discrimination, and poverty. Still, when we are backed into our minds' darkest corners, we are not ill or in need of help, we are Latina. We are our mothers' daughters.

The internet will tell you it's true. There is an endless stream of content detailing how Latinas are violent, hysterical, melodramatic, fiery, spicy. How dating a Latina is a death sentence. How it takes a certain kind of man to tame a Latina. In this way, we are magnified and minimized, made hyper-visible and invisible, made into two-dimensional irrational creatures

that shouldn't be taken seriously. We are reduced to bodies that must be controlled.

I started the majority of these poems when I was an undergrad at an overwhelmingly white university. I was furiously unwell, in the throes of an untreated eating disorder and undiagnosed bipolar disorder, trying my hardest to suppress who I was, and trying my hardest to pass as a quiet, unemotional, unMexican girl. I was none of those things.

I finished most of these poems after realizing the "a" at the end of Latina does not fit me. This was also after I got help, got medicated, learned to see myself as a person instead of a body, and found things to like about the person I was. It was after Lora's murder– which had gone unsolved for nearly 40 years– was reopened.

In 2022, it was concluded that former deputy Jim Harrison had abducted, sexually assaulted, and killed Lora. By the time of this discovery, Harrison had been dead for 25 years. My idea of what it looked like to be a good girl was long-shattered by this point, but Harrison's identification as the murderer made it all that much clearer. Being a good girl was worth nothing in a world that did not see our bodies as capable of holding anything good. To be a good girl, one has to believe in the good guys and the good guys, the deputies, wanted us dead.

I'm tired of carrying all of the blame and the curses and the evil within me. I wrote this book to say that it is not ours to carry. Not mine, not Lora's, not the memory of Lora, or the women tucking it into their stories. It never was. This book is a letting go

Nen G Ramirez

MISS AMERICA

*"When these southern whites see these
pretty Mexican girls, they become excited—
they are not used to girls so pretty."*
EYEWITNESS ON THE ZOOT SUIT RIOTS

My mom was 16
when her boss's khakis fell to his knees

while he waited with a smile
for her in the Domino's freezer

to see her scared,
waiting to say, 'don't be.'

He had seen her

thick Selena lips
& J-Lo hips.

He'd heard about girls like her.

My sister was 15
when a rusted pickup followed her

all the way home,
driver whistling,

dreaming out loud
of fistfuls

of her long dark hair.

My cousin was 11
when her body was found

                                        naked & hollow in a ditch.

                    The whole neighborhood
                    sighed,

        said she was always
        too pretty.

They engraved *Miss America* into her headstone.

EXAMPLES OF THE CRAZY LATINA™

1. My aunt dragging her husband's mistress across a bar floor by her hair
2. My mother using other women's panties to kindle a fire in her boyfriend's kitchen sink
3. My mother throwing hot coffee at my stepfather after he called my sister a little bitch
4. My mother pushing my stepfather down the stairs when he cornered her, fist raised
5. My mother telling my grandparents that she was raped
6. My younger sister skipping school because some days she can't stand the sun
7. My older sister swearing she's been dead for three days
8. Me googling the number of calories in bleach

ON SUNDAYS, SHE'D MAKE MY ABUELO LENGUA

like they had back home because they were
only a dollar since the butcher would throw them out
anyway. She'd cook it all night, and when they
got back from church, she'd shred
the tender meat, pile it on
corn tortillas, serve it to her Chuy, con limón,
and they would recite the same stories
about the same bars: the floors sticky
and them, young and uncaring. They'd repeat
names and places and roll their r's so
their tongues wouldn't forget.

But when the butcher tried
to charge her $20 for a tongue, saying,
It's a delicacy for you guys, isn't it?
My abuela left empty-handed, wanting
to curse him, unable
to find the words.

I TELL MY ABUELA I GOT MY FIRST PERIOD

and she makes me té de canela,
teaches me how to leach
the bitterness from bark, then
soften rust-red water with milk and sugar,
turning it the soft sad pink
of overcast sunset
she hands me the steaming cup
and says this ache means
I get to have daughters
who will get to ache too.

I gulp it fast and burn my throat and imagine all the daughters inside me
boiling away

MY MOTHER FINDS MY FIRST BLOOD-STAINED PANTIES

and buys us a bottle of Strawberry Hill,
says she's waited so long for me to feel her hurt

shows me how peroxide bubbles blood from clothes
how pillows smother the sharpest cries
how ice shrinks eyelids swollen shut

says *Baby, this is what it's all about*

and from the fridge, takes out a cake
with a cursive buttercream *bienvenidas*,
        she cuts me a slice and
        I throw the whole plate away

PIOJOSA

My abuelito says you aren't really
Mexican-American until you've had piojos.

My mother says you aren't really
Mexican-American until you can't get rid of piojos.

It's hard to forget the sound of a louse
exoskeleton cracking between your

thumb nails and gushing its blood/
your blood over your palm. You

aren't until you bake and melt the synthetic
fibers of your favorite sweaters in the dryer,

or sleep with a scalp smothered in mayonnaise
or olive oil or vinegar, or until

you can't tell if you are killing the pests or
marinating them to perfection.

You aren't really Mexican-American
until you've given up and love the beast

that's sucking you dry.

THE FIRST PANIC
ATTACK

I was 15 when I first said goodbye to this world
then found myself lying naked
on the cardiologist's table
breasts slathered in ultrasound blue goo
15 when I was high for the first time:
my stepfather's painkillers
dusty in a ziplock baggie

I cried *Please*
my heart is stuck
in the garbage disposal, deep, rattling
around, caught with a fork

it took me two months to wrestle
it out–shredded, moldy, and
tangled with ramen

STARBUCKS PSEUDONYM

The barista asks for my name and I say Maria. Maria, every time. Maria leaves no room for mispronunciation or *Can you spell that?* Everyone knows Maria. She's never questioned, she is the answer to every question. All those ugly *What are you* and *What kind* questions. Maria is familiar, puts their minds at rest. Maria is probably Catholic. Maria comes from a big family, works hard, respects her elders. She's Crunchwrap Supreme meal with mild sauce. Dora the Explorer and Handy Manny before school and Maya and Miguel after. The radio edit of Despacito. Maria is not *María*. She does not roll the r and doesn't expect you to either. Maria never asks too much. Maria is happy to be here.

LOVE SONG FOR LA LLORONA

I have been you, Llorona,
in the back of classrooms and
sprawled out on the sidewalk,
stringy black hair,
sharpie-colored fingernails and
chewed up hoodie strings
crystallized with spit.

I am you, Llorona.
All women are born wailing,
you and I just never stopped,
we were meant to curse everything we touch,
to cry Where have all the children gone?

I lost them too, Llorona.
You won't need to steal me in the night,
I'll gladly walk with you and call
Mis hijos
Mis hijas
Mis hermanas
Mis primas
Mis amigas

Sweet scabby-kneed girls
now younger than me,
god help us find
all we let die.

BEFORE YOUR COUSIN LORA WAS A THREAT, SHE WAS A GIRL

Before she was a poem, she was alive.

The story always goes like this:

a pretty brown girl
exists too much
and ends up dead.

The good man was
the bad man was
the devil was
the deputy.

In most versions of the story,
the girl is walking to a home
she shouldn't have left.

Before these words were mine,
they were my mother's

and her mother's
and everyone's mothers'.

In every version they are sorry.

I hope that when you're older you will
understand enough to forgive me.

I hope even more that you don't.

WOW YOU LOOK JUST LIKE

Are you related?

MY BABY SISTER ASKS ME WHAT WITHDRAWAL MEANS, AND I DON'T SAY:

It means I can cry on command because I'm more or less always pressing my back
to the door and also that Lexapro was a good lover that I can no longer afford.
It means trying to suppress suicidal fantasies like church-coughs.
It means day-old tortillas sitting on the stove, fossilizing,
body feeling like some freezer-burnt Wednesday
microwaved, bloated, reheated-gooey.
It means lucky sweater every day, and
ice water meets empty stomach.
It means lately I'm all guts.

IN THE PRODUCE AISLE, A WOMAN TELLS ME TO GO BACK TO MEXICO AND I

A.   ask her to repeat herself. She says, "I said you're a total smokeshow." I blush and give her my number. We go out for drinks. Frozen margs and pictures of her dog. She ghosts me.

B.   ask her to repeat herself. She says, "I said to go back to Mexico." I thank her for her patience, explain that my hearing is bad. She says, "You can't help it."

C.   say I've never been to Mexico and she recommends this resort in Cancun where the workers treat you like family. She says it's gorgeous this time of year.

D.   ask her why she's so angry. We sit and discuss her piece-of-work boss and messy divorce. Turns out she's a total Monica and I'm such a Phoebe that she invites me to her crochet club.

E.   knock out the bitch's lights and become a Crazy Latina meme on Facebook, a debate on Reddit, and a bullet-point in the next shooter's manifesto.

SELF-PORTRAIT AS COYOLXAUHQUI

1.
Or rather Koyochowski:
another nonsense name
for how I inherited Ramirez hair
And my Polish grandma pays
for me to get it thinned.

2.
I am more border than body,
not quite brown but still
butchered.

My stomach lies in the East side
when it's as empty
as my mother's pockets.

My stomach belongs to the cul-de-sac
when I skip meals for a white boy.
The frijoles se enfrían,
Abuela butter-tubs them for me,
sends me off with a sana, sana.

3.

I remember watching Selena on a cracked VHS tape–
Selena on the roof of her house, staring up at the moon,
Suzette climbs up and asks, *What are you doing?*
Selena smiles and says, *I'm dreaming*.

4.

I leave home for the city,
I study astronomy and stand
on top of Liberty Parking Structure
with a girl I think I could fall
in love with or someday call
sister, and stare at the moon. I've never
dreamt of being anywhere so tall.
I've never imagined so long a fall.

5.

A year later with body carved and hollowed,
my sleepdrunk feet carry me to Liberty
almost every night.

I dream of jumping head first.
I dream that instead of a splat I become
a satellite: an hija, a nieta, better loved
from a distance. Demi-dead and still
bleeding, revolving, reflecting back
all I could have been.

6.

I run into the girl at a party.
She holds a boy's hand and says my name
is on the tip of her tongue.

7.

Here's something I learned:
Each lava-bleeding wound on the moon--
They're all named Maria.

LATINA GFS BE LIKE: A COMEDY SKETCH BY LELE PONS

Stop me if you've heard this one before: a white Latina with only two moods-- Takis and arson. It's not easy being so chisme her chanclas have no chill yet copping an attitude so thicc it's wifey material, and still she finds the panties/earring/lipstick of some other puta in her man's room/car/couch cushion. Ay ay ay the chingadopendejohijodediablo. So she chases him with a [kitchen utensil], throws his [electronic] out the window, and calls her ex-con primos (Junior, Junior, and Junior) but oops! It was just a misunderstanding! He's harmless! She's spicy! They kiss to Gasolina or Mas Maiz or Suavemente and todos somos felices. It's so fun to be out of control when you're not so deep under it, to be savage when the word is such a distant memory. And just think how empowered that brown Latina must feel when her lover claims she forced his hand, calls her "psycho bitch," how she'd spit bloodied molars and say, "Yes! Yes! You know! Us Latinas! We're crazy!"

IN THE CAFÉ MY EX SAYS HE DOESN'T HAVE A TYPE

I know she had a habit of lying in the street
and he fell in love with her in the headlights
of a semi-truck that didn't kill her
but could have if she decided
the game was over

he says she was fucking crazy
I say I used to play the same game
and he says, *Trust me*
you aren't like her

I don't say that I understood the pleasure
of wheels rattling my chest
and feeling the weak organ that cares
jerk awake

he says he doesn't know
if he'll ever understand her
I don't talk about my suspicion that

she and I lived the same life
origami-ed ourselves into the same polite shapes
to seduce the white boy with clean sneakers and baby fat
because there are as many bland boys
looking for manic pixie dream girls
as pill-bitter girls looking for someone
to miss and eulogize them

I ask how was the funeral
he says he wouldn't know
he didn't have the tears
or the words

So I say take mine
I've kept them warm.

MY MOTHER IS SIXTEEN AND MY ABUELA WONDERS WHY SHE HASN'T HAD TO BUY TAMPONS

when my mother says she can't keep it, she is crazy
when my mother says she loves it, she is crazy

but when she wakes up drenched in blood,
she is quiet

stays in bed
all day

my abuela whistles while doing laundry
returns my mother's sheets folded and bleached
and says, *god works in mysterious ways*

I AM EIGHTEEN AND MY MOTHER WONDERS WHY SHE HASN'T HAD TO BUY TAMPONS

my period left without a goodbye
or a chance for me to say sorry
after years of starving myself prepubescent
what should I have expected besides
my body's silent treatment
a maternal passive aggression
an icy withholding

as much as I want to kneel
before an open fridge and
soften myself with milk and sugar--
I am too tired and heavy
with this new ache

to who could have been
mis Marias, mis Esperanzas, mis Doloritas:
I'm sorry
but close the door behind you
Mami just wants to rest today
I have nothing
to spare, can't bring
myself to need
or be needed

RIME OF MY MOTHER

She microwaved her puppy
but only because she was a child
and because the puppy was frozen solid.

She wanted only to undo a different evil—
the dog forgotten among snow and mist.
Her own mother helped her bury the body
but couldn't look at her for days.

Tequilabreathed and glittereyed,

my mother recites this story to
every quinceañera, never

getting to the ooze of it but

afterwards
sleeps soundly and bucketside
as I wonder if
for a second
the puppy's bloating
belly looked to her like
resurrection.

MOVING IN

"I don't mean to cause alarm
but I think there's an alligator in the basement,"
I tell my mother on our first day spent
scrubbing what was once our home,
then her ex husband's,
and now ours again.

So my mother creeps down
creaking stairs, shines
her iphone flashlight
into the dark cavity of a house
that once again
felt haunted.

       Yes, he moved in a different woman
       with new kids who resented him
       in new ways,
       left the carpet
       with new stains.

She takes a good long look
when she finds it in the corner
and texts the man who once loved her
Did you lose a cat?

He says a kitten ran away,
But that was years ago.
She lifts the thing
by its rigid tail:
mummified, yellow, scaled,
and two feet
long at least.
This isn't
a kitten
anymore.

And her heart chills at the thought
of the man she loved before
(she learned to prepare liver for him,
started wearing seatbelts, even)
shedding himself of us, all the skin
she knew, turning to dust. How he lived
this life with his family of strangers:
slamming doors, breaking dishes,
burning dinner, oblivious
to the kitten—

Trapped, too weak
to scratch,
in the dark, turning
into cat and then corpse
and, now, alligator.
That the man thought
it was free, probably

even happy, running the streets
and fucking in parking lots,
if he ever thought of it
at all.

IN MY COUNTRY

the streets are lined with gold-
plated hoops tossed aside the night before.
The sea shimmers like glass
shattered from windshields.

Here, acrylics only come stilettoed.
Mamacitas only come mercurial.

In my country, there is no night
without a thousand slashed tires
and there is no morning
without deflated women
asking you to fill them.

Where I'm from, we have no need
for sun or moon because
women are always burning
some cabron's shit in some backyard.

The women burn
and beg to be held,

and don't all white boys have a bit
of a pyromaniac streak?
And don't we make you feel brave?
And don't you think
it's better that way?

POC BOOK
COVER MODEL

I am faceless, forever facing
a solid, bright background
that seduces preteens
at the Scholastic fair. My long
black-as-licorice braids with their
sweet virginal shine beg for
pity, are maybe a metaphor
for tradition, repression, machismo,
all the miserable Mexican girls that need
to be saved from Mexican men.

I've portrayed all kinds
of Mexicans: Puerto Ricans,
Guatemalans, Peruvians, and even
a few Chinese. It's easy when you're
faceless: all smooth, tan skin
and thick hair, for a few blue
moon romance novels,
a wide set of hips.

Most days are a dream.
My fiancé says I'm effortless
to love, the way I am

modest and mute and not
too dark, how when he presses
his palm to the plane
of my skin, its indent
remains like modeling clay.

Other days, I know
the eyes are burning
through the back of my head,
and for a sure second, a pair
of my own burning within
it. If I were to tear
away this caramel-colored
membrane to find those
eyes blue and lashes pale or
to find just orificeless pulp,
I might just keep digging.

GHAZAL TO THE TUNE OF "LA HIJA DE NADIE"

My mother and I cry to the same ranchera song.
We share the same salt-and-lime running-mascara song.

Las hijas de nadie. Both cry with Yolanda del
Río. Both bled dry for kind eyes, a father, a song.

We have both danced on sticky bar floors with a stranger
or handsy primo to the same Reagan-era song.

Each time she drinks she gets a new tattoo of lovers' names,
then cries in the car with her speakers blaring our song.

Every doomed path turns blue under my mother's skin—
raised and inked over, a bulging pained prayer, a song.

I've grown into her mania, watched her freckles spot
my shoulders and hips that sway to the same guera song.

Whoever dies first wins those sorrowful trumpets and
gritos as their reunion-con-la-tierra song.

The doctor says to bury my mother. Mourn for who
I needed and love who I have, the one who shares the song.

After all the pillow-choked sobs, Baby-teeth slapped from
bloody gums, we still cry to the same ranch'era song.

WHEN I WAS 12 I WAS A FOLKLORICO DANCER

Which is to say I learned femininity
as performance

I learned Revlon Very Cherry
Blackest Black MegaLiner
Lavender Smoke Shadow and
Plumberry Instant Cheekbones

black yarn braid and
silk flowers fastened
to my scalp and fake
gold chandelier earrings
that always came out
crusted in blood

I learned that being a girl
was something to make
them see from the back row

and still I found myself
practicing the boy parts in my garage
picturing me on stage
in the pants with gold buttons
all the way down the legs, how I'd
crescent moon my body around
my partner—her sea of skirt
crests and curls

I pictured how I'd take her hand,
twirl her into my chest, tilt
my sombrero to mask
a kiss, because it's just
for us—our falsies fluttering
against each other and
lipstick smearing: all of this,
ours

ABECEDARIAN IN WHICH LA CHILLONA USES HER WORDS

Abuelo asks me whenever I cry *are you a man or a mouse*
but Abuela knows I am neither   I am mother of everything   of each
caterpillar collected in paper cup   of all the baby
dandelion heads popped prematurely from
each milky blooded stem-neck   I'll
funeral each and every one of them
give a sandbox burial and ten
Hail Marys at least   I'll pray for every
innocent and voiceless soft-souled thing
just like Abuela and her tortillas swaddled in
kitchen towels until they taste
like lavender baby wash   just like each storybook
mouse and bunny I kiss goodnight on their watercolor
noses   just like all the pinto beans I sort
one by one on the plastic-lined kitchen table   making a
pile for the ugly ones   the shriveled ones   even my
querido dirtclumps and pebbles are special and deserving and
reserved for loteria   I am the mother of the whole card (la
Sirena   el Pajaro   la Rana   el Borracho) and love
them all the same (even if el Valiente doesn't call home so much) and

38

unconditionally   they're allowed to cry   I'd never force them to raise their voice over the music   stand in

front of the whole party   apologize

when one of their caterpillars falls from cup and bloodbursts beneath Tía

Ximena's heel (who doesn't apologize, never loved that caterpillar, only cries over its mess)

yes I always answer *man* but want to be the mouse (paper   soft   sipping tea) or muñeca or her

zapatitos or bottle or its milk   disappearing when tilted into dollmouth thank god it

disappears

AT THE PARTY, MY ANXIETY TUGS ON MY PANT LEG

I look down and see her all red-faced snot-sleeved squirming stomping and threatening a storm so I scoop her up and tell my friends it's getting late but we should do this again soon and after she howls and thrashes the whole way home and after I wash her trembling back and brush her hair I lull her to sleep but when I am lying in bed she climbs in and curls up next to me and won't lie still and in the faint light of the lamp she makes shadow puppets of a snarling hound and a crocodile's snapping jaw.

All night long, with the hands I gave her, she makes monsters out of thin air.

ON AFTERPARTY PUKING

This time there are no scratched
throats or bloodied
fingernails, just your
muscles' rhythmic squeeze
knowing what to do, how to
pour out all the ways
I've tried to kill you, all that
I've flooded you with after
keeping you empty for so long.

Thank you, body, for handling
the dirty work, for letting me be
a log bobbing in the waves
of necessary motion, letting me
doze off passenger-side.

Thank you for trying to be okay
even after all the times I've packed
a bag, said *I'm running away*. You let me
stand at the door, knowing I wouldn't, then
let me crumble, cry. You said *Just
let it out, just rest*.
I don't think I'll ever understand

your love for me: a rum-dumb
brain like a snot-bubbling toddler who
throws books from the shelf, throws
punches, screams *I hate you*,
        and still: You put everything
        in its place, bathe me, tuck me in, leave
        the door cracked,
        the hallway light on.

BEFORE THEY WERE FOUND

for V

I don't know how many
more times I'll be able to handle
the words "she was found."

V, we were both born afraid
of ditches, the unseen evil
hissing in weeds and muck.

We'd bike down gravel roads
to St. Agnes just to see her
head stone, *Lora Huizar*
> *(1972-1983)*
> *"Miss America"*

We'd pray for and to her.

Dragged by our hair, our moms
taught us about la llorona,
el cucuy, and the ditch.

And still we both grew up
thinking we could outrun our blood,
outlive our weeping name.

We fell in love easy,
snuck out of bedroom windows,
rode in drunk boys' cars.

He tossed you out with garbage, leaking life.

The cops said "we found her"
like you only existed once
they chanced upon your empty

body beside the road,
abandoned, mosquito-bitten, and
collecting sweet dew.

You were not brought to light.

We've been the light the entire time.

LORENA BOBBITT AS COYOLXAUHQUI

If we are to speak
of the severing,
to remember the dis
and re-membering,
let it be
of Lorena,
every piece
of her made
separate and scattered:
the acetone the spandex the fridge light

let us revision her full as the moon

because
when he held her
by the wrists
over the balcony
she was quiet inside
knowing if he let go
she'd float
away, whole,

untouched
by anything
 but sky

46

READING GUIDE

Internet and Pop Culture

Now more than ever, the internet and pop culture infiltrate every aspect of our lives, but the scarcity of representation of Latinx people has arguably remained consistent. One of the most common representations of Latinas has been The Crazy Latina, featured as a joke in sitcoms and movies and now as a very popular meme. The Crazy Latina is everywhere, and especially in the poems, "In the produce aisle, a woman tells me to go back to Mexico and I," "Latina GFs Be Like: A Comedy Sketch by Lele Pons," and, of course, "Examples of the Crazy Latina." These poems seek to reveal the danger behind the meme and the harm that it causes.

- How has pop culture depicted your identity?
- How has it shaped the way you view or have viewed your own identity?
- Write a poem that borrows an internet form (a meme, a Twitter thread, a Reddit post, etc)

Stereotype

The Crazy Latina is an example of a stereotype which paints Latinas as inherently violent, loud, and unstable. Additionally, the stereotype of Latinas as submissive can be found in "POC Book Cover Model" and "Starbucks Pseudonym." The women in these poems fit into the claustrophobic gender role of "marianismo," and this stereotype is also fetishized. These stereotypes reduce Latinas to sexual objects, unreliable narrators, and unwanted narrators.

- Have you ever been flattened into a stereotype?
- Have you ever judged yourself based on whether you fit into a stereotype or not?
- If this two-dimensional stereotype could speak, what would they say to you?
- What would you say to them?

The Body

T he idea of eating disorders and discomfort in one's body is an under-
current that runs through this collection. Restrictive eating and purging is
implied in the poems, "My mother finds my first blood-stained panties," "I
am eighteen and my mother wonders why she hasn't had to buy tampons,"
and "On Afterparty Puking." We've seen in these poems the way that Latina
bodies are sexualized, policed, and brutalized. We've also seen the ways that
memory is inherited and carried within our bodies through generations.

- How have factors of race and class affected your relationship
  to your body?
- What histories does your body carry?
- Write a love letter to a part of your body that you've
  struggled with.

ACKNOWLEDGMENTS

This book would not be possible without the love and support of my amazing partner, Connor Jessee. You are my favorite thing about me.

To Inocencia, my sister and best friend, thank you for the gorgeous cover art and for keeping me breathing. We've lived a life.

Huge thanks to Laura Kasischke– my mentor, advisor, and hero– for the immense amount of guidance and support she gave me while writing these poems.

So much love and appreciation for my incredible and brilliant friends who nurtured me and these poems during our darkest days: Hannah Boettcher Olson, Sarah Hamilton, Katie Miller, Nadia Mota, and Jordan Young.

I am so grateful to my professors at the University of Minnesota MFA program, especially Douglas Kearney and Kate Nuernberger, and all of my friends I've made there. I especially want to thank the members of my cohort: Ciara Alfaro, Jon Crowl, Olivia Fantini, Brandon Hackbarth, and Gregory Langen for being such generous, kind, and supportive readers and friends. I love you all so much it hurts.

A special shoutout to my fantastic editor, Michaela Mullin, for all of her energy, care, and time. Thank you for believing in these poems and helping me believe in them too.

Thank you to my younger siblings, Chente and Razor Blade, to whom I owe everything.

So much gratitude to torrin a. greathouse, Shannon McLeod, Kyle Prue, and Octavio Quintanilla for the overwhelmingly kind blurbs they provided for this book.

Thank you to my family and to all Huizar and Ramirez women. Thank you to all my trans, queer, punk, emo, and Mexican family I've found in Minnesota.

Thank you, Dr. Kong. Thank you, Mohamed. Thank you, Morning Fresh Bakery. Thank you, Paige. Thank you, Kirsten. Thank you, reader. Thank you so much.

Lastly, I want to thank the following publications for publishing earlier versions of these poems:

Acentos Review: "Miss America" and "Piojosa"

GASHER Journal: "In the Café My Ex Says He Doesn't Have a Type"

Quarterly West: "Moving In"

Electric Literature: "In my country" and "POC Book Cover Model"

Academy of American Poets: "Abecedarian in Which la Chillona Uses Her Words"

Nen G Ramirez

Nen G Ramirez is a Chicanx writer from Adrian, Michigan. They are an MFA candidate at the University of Minnesota whose work has appeared in *Acentos Review*, *Split Lip Magazine*, *Poetry Magazine*, and elsewhere.

4 OTHER WAYS TO
SUPPORT
NOMADIC PRESS
WRITERS

Please consider supporting these funds. You can donate on a one-time or monthly basis from $10–∞ You can also more generally support Nomadic Press by donating to our general fund via nomadicpress. org/donate and by continuing to buy our books.

As always, thank you for your support!

Scan the QR code for more information and/or to donate.

You can also donate at nomadicpress.org/store.

ABOUT THE FUNDS

XALAPA
FUND

XALAPA FUND

The Xalapa Fund was started in May of 2022 to help offset the airfare costs of Nomadic Press authors to travel to our new retreat space in Xalapa, Veracruz in Mexico. Funds of up to $350 will be dispersed to any Nomadic Press published author who wishes to travel to Xalapa. The funds are kept in a separate bank account and disbursements are overseen by three (3) Nomadic Press authors and Founding Publisher J. K. Fowler.

Inherent in these movements will be cultural exchanges and Nomadic Press will launch a reading series based out of the bookstore/cafe downstairs from the space in August 2022. This series will feature Xalapa-based writers and musicians as well as open-mic slots and will be live streamed to build out relationships between our communities in Oakland, California, Philadelphia, Pennsylvania, and the greater US (and beyond).

EMERGENCY FUND

Right before Labor Day 2020 (and in response to the effects of COVID), Nomadic Press launched its Emergency Fund, a forever fund meant to support Nomadic Press-published writers who have no income, are unemployed, don't qualify for unemployment, have no healthcare, or are just generally in need of covering unexpected or impactful expenses.

Funds are first come, first serve, and are available as long as there is money in the account, and there is a dignity centered internal application that interested folks submit. Disbursements are made for any amount up to $300. All donations made to this fund are kept in a separate account. The Nomadic Press Emergency Fund (NPEF) account and associated processes (like the application) are overseen by Nomadic Press authors and the group meets every month.

BLACK WRITERS FUND

On Juneteenth (June 19) 2020, Nomadic Press launched the Nomadic Press Black Writers Fund (NPBWF), a forever fund that will be directly built into the fabric of our organization for as long as Nomadic Press exists and puts additional monies directly into the pockets of our Black writers at the end of each year.

Here is how it works: $1 of each book sale goes into the fund. At the end of each year, all Nomadic Press authors have the opportunity to voluntarily donate none, part, or all of their royalties to the fund. Anyone from our larger communities can donate to the fund. This is where you come in! At the end of the year, whatever monies are in the fund will be evenly distributed to all Black Nomadic Press authors that have been published by the date of disbursement (mid-to-late December). The fund (and associated, separate bank account) has an oversight team comprised of four authors (Ayodele Nzinga, Daniel B. Summerhill, Dazié Grego-Sykes, and Odelia Younge) + Nomadic Press Executive Director J. K. Fowler.

PAINTING THE STREETS FUND

The Nomadic Press Painting the Streets Fund was launched in February 2022 to support visual arts programs in Oakland flatlands' schools. Its launch coincided with the release of *Painting the Streets: Oakland Uprising in the Time of Rebellion*. Your donations here will go directly into a separate bank account overseen by J. K. Fowler (Nomadic Press), Elena Serrano (Eastside Arts Alliance), Leslie Lopez (EastSide Arts Alliance), Rachel Wolfe-Goldsmith (BAMP), and Andre Jones (BAMP). In addition, all net proceeds from the sale of *Painting the Streets: Oakland Uprising in the Time of Rebellion* will go into this fund. We will share the fund's impact annually on project partner websites. Here are a few schools that we have already earmarked to receive funds: Ile Omode, Madison High School, McClymonds High School, Roosevelt Middle School, Elmhurst Middle School, Castlemont High School, Urban Promise Academy, West Oakland Middle School, and POC Homeschoolers of Oakland.